GW00384215

OLD BARRY
IN PHOTOGRAPHS

1 *(overleaf)* Cadoxton 'Old Village' *c.*1914 grew up around St Cadoc's Church from which it takes its name. The church consists of a chancel and nave, western saddleback tower and large south porch. It is first recorded in 1254 when as 'Caddokeston' it paid 7 marks, 9 shillings and 4 pence towards the crusade of Henry III. The adjoining *Three Bells Inn*, so called in 1841, derives its name from the three bells in the church tower cast in 1826 by T. Mears of Whitechapel. Two were cracked prior to 1895, and the third, still in use, was recast in 1931

Old BARRY in photographs

WITH COMMENTARIES BY
BRIAN C. LUXTON

FOREWORD BY GWYN THOMAS

STEWART WILLIAMS

Barry

First published September, 1977
© Stewart Williams, Publishers,
Bryn Awel, Buttrills Road,
Barry, South Glamorgan.

ISBN 0 900807 25 3

ACKNOWLEDGMENTS

I would like to thank the following for giving their kind permission to use their photographs: Mrs M. Ashton (9, 10, 33, 115); Barry Athletic Club (63); Barry Boys' Comprehensive School (122, 123); *Barry & District News* (54, 64, 86, 114, 125, 126, 129); Barry Docks Offices (189);   Barry Public Library (5, 16, 17, 18, 45, 52, 60, 65, 85, 98, 130, 144, 153, 154, 155); Barry Rugby Club (58, 59); Barry Yacht Club (68); Tudor E. Brock (15); A. Cramp (159); Mrs J. G. Card (38); T. Clemett (66); W. B. Carpenter, whose postcards are from plates by Heber Shirvington (37, 41, 43, 84, 106, 139, 169, 170, 171, 172, 173, 174, 175, 176, 177, 178, 179, 180, 181, 182, 192, 194, 197); Mrs A. M. Clissold (29); R. Coombs (69); V. A. Corbin (56, 92, 145, 148, 149, 150, 151, 152, 157, 158); C. R. Croome (97, 135, 136, 137, 138, 156); R. H. Dally (28); Mrs I. Davies (39); W. M. Davies (13); Ivor R. Day (132); Alcwyn Evans (91); L. J. Gardiner (133); M. Greener (95); Miss E. F. Head (124); Mrs D. Horgan (40); G. Howe (82); Mrs V. Hutton (31); E. H. Incledon (70); F. C. John, who loaned the following Shirvington glass plates (14, 20, 32, 35, 42, 46, 47, 49, 50, 55, 67, 77, 78, 79, 81, 100, 101, 102, 113, 117, 118, 120, 121, 128, 146, 183, 184, 185, 186, 187, 188, 190, 191, 195, 196, 200); B. W. Jones (93); J. L. Jones (73); R. J. Lewis (61, 94); B. C. Luxton (3, 6, 12, 24, 26, 30, 44, 48, 71, 76, 80, 96, 99, 105, 108, 131, 140, 163, 167, 193); O. T. May (83); J. O'Sullivan (134); A. Pittard-Davies (7, 8, 160, 161, 162, 164); Mrs E. Phipps (72); H. Press (89, 90); Mrs M. Pugh (1, frontispiece); Mrs E. Randall (11); Miss M. Read (127); E. Rees (147, 168); W. E. Rogers (74); J. M. Rowlands (88); St Mary's Church (109); A. Saunders (119); R. Sterio (4, 21, 23, 25, 111); J. Stevens (2, 27, 36, 51, 62, 75, 104, 112, 116, 141, 165, 166, 198, 199); G. D. Thomas (143); K. B. Thomas (142); T. J. Thomas (57); T. Trought (53); H. Ventris-Jenkins (19, 34, 107, 110); Miss G. Williams (22, 87); J. Yeandle (103).

I would also like to thank Viv Corbin for his valuable assistance with the section on Communications, John Doughty of Barry Camera Club, Chris Taylor, Haydn T. Baynham, A. Pittard-Davies and Gwyn Thomas for kindly agreeing to write the foreword.

B.C.L.

Printed in Wales by D. Brown and Sons Ltd., Cowbridge and Bridgend

FOREWORD
by GWYN THOMAS

the celebrated author, playwright and television personality

ARRY IS AS INTERESTING a stretch of 20th century landscape as one is likely to see in Britain. The town in its modern form blew into being as one of the last bursts of the volcanic energy that brought Britain through the last century and up to the First World War.

When Cardiff Docks were established it was done under the canopy of Bute wealth and prestige. The Middle Ages were still around. Barry belonged to an age of new men and new drives. David Davies of Llandinam, by Bute standards, was an urchin, a creature in whom the hungry frustrations of the young peasant rose to a peak of constructive genius.

He sank deeper pits than anyone else and assembled an army of engineers and navvies to build a port which was to become, for its brief historical day, the world's capital of coal for sale. If all the coal handled by Barry could be raised in one vast heap it could be represented in two simple symbols, a sea of sweat or a pyramid of gold. That, and a thousand hills to the north of the Vale of Glamorgan, made hollow and tetchy by millions of delvers who created out of their toil a whole new resonant civilisation.

Lord Davies's family gave generously to the building of a Memorial Hall to record and cherish the men of Barry who died on active service. It is the whole epoch and spirit of men like David Davies that now needs commemoration and requires our curious research. He and Barry sprang from a time when enterprise, investment and labour flowed in golden floods. Many of the photographs in this book, of big men digging big holes and handling big ships, speak of an age of brazen confidence.

If anyone had ever whispered that one day, not too distant, dust would settle on some of their proudest achievements, they would have dismissed the prophet as a loon.

The demolisher's ball has sailed through their most solemn aspirations. The muscle that made the docks gives way to the ingenuity of advanced science and physically smaller ploys. A significant chemical works stands near the site of the docks. There is a statue of Lord Davies in the county of his birth in mid-Wales. He is seen looking pensive and studying a blueprint, probably of a mine or a harbour. The statue, not knowing about the colour of the print, has turned green. It somehow sums up an age and a philosophy that, for a time at least, have lost their first divine puff.

Lord Davies today would be in chemicals, probably not even in Britain. One can see him as a multi-national, even a multi-planetary giant, making aspirin for Martians worried bilious about men or vegetable tonics for Venusians working up courage to guard their corner of space against TV companies mad for new locations.

The drama of Barry for me has two wonderful aspects. Past its harbour walls went the mineral dragged from beneath the mountains where I lived. And at the town's edge was a miraculously preserved enclave of pleasure and amenity. South Wales exported its coal and half-exported its children, for many of the hordes of children, who came down from the valleys under the banners of their Sunday Schools, must often have felt, thinking of the grey snakes of uniform hillside housing from which they had come, that they would have liked to continue the pilgrimage of freedom that had brought them as far as Whitmore Bay.

The marshalling of the faithful in numberless vestries for the annual trip to Barry Island must provide one of the most piquant footnotes in the history of Christianity. The suitcases in which the sandwiches were brought to the feast were the brittlest things in the whole range of synthetic saddlery. The locks were God's gift to Raffles, and it was no time before the sands between Nell's Point and Friar's Point were white with spilled sandwiches. The addition of sand to the filling was no impediment. The sand was shaken off the titbits and we were ordered harshly to pitch in and be thankful.

For seconds on end the sound of sad, gritty chewing would dim the strains of 'Let a Smile be your Umbrella on a Rainy, Rainy Day' being played on the fairground organ. We swallowed so much sand it gave our metabolism an Arabian bray and almost led a few of us to be racially reclassified.

The fairground was a finer, deeper mystery than the strange social conflicts and cultural jousts of our mining towns. As I walk around the Island now wisps of old experience, some pathetic, some farcical, move around in a wind of remembering.

In those lean days bathing costumes were never taken on the outing because we never had them. They were an idiotic novelty. Had we possessed any such thing we would have bought a matching tie and treated it as a separate suit. We hired costumes from a depot that stood where the paddling pool is now. Age had pulled these garments miles out of their original shape, and when we came forth, ready for action, we looked a little like Batman but not as neat. Out of shyness we stuck close together as we made for the water, often in Indian file, humming any one of the many funeral chants that made up a large part of our valley's musical effects.

The coconut shies had a magnetic pull for miners whose shoulders had the breadth and development of Charles Atlas. One of our number, George, was a gigantic rugby forward who put so many opponents in hospital he had a fracture ward in the Lower Rhondda named after him. Within minutes of getting off the train, George would be aiming at the coconuts. He always promised us an armful each when he had flattened the shy. This was going to be the peak of the treat. We kept our arms free for the loot. The balls came bouncing off the nuts like electrons. A few spectators were bruised by balls bouncing

back from the targets but the nuts did not budge. The nuts either had iron kernels or rested in nests of magnetic sawdust.

George never won a nut. Once when his chagrin led him into a murderous mood and he threatened, as revenge, to steal one of the donkeys that trotted along the beach, the superintendent of the Sunday School took him away from the Island to show him some of Barry's other faces. There was the pebble beach at Cold Knap, still undeveloped. No rowing lake, bathing pool, Bindles or promenade.

The superintendent, a scholarly man, took the thrower to have a look at the residual Norman Castle in what is now the Garden Suburb. 'Those Normans', said the superintendent, 'Believed in marking the earth. Their buildings were tied to the very roots of time'. 'Like those so-and-so coconuts', said George.

The Figure 8, as I knew it, is no longer there. Back home we were nourished in our chapels and political rallies on lurid declamations. At one moment, a tormented reformer would be promising you hell in the next life. An hour later some sanguine political demagogue would be telling you that heaven on earth would be rolling in on the next bus. Coming on top of this dialectical switchback the Figure 8 finished us off. Our contingent always included the chapel's First Aid Group and one of this team would be detailed to keep an eye on chapel members, with frail nerves and tricky stomachs, driven into despair and delirium by the alarming dips and climbs of the Figure 8.

Coming to a later time I recall a sideshow in which a group of cannibals were being exhibited. There were about ten of them, snarling, snorting, shaking spears and wearing what looked like little more than two primly placed Shredded Wheats. The show's barker was in full cry. 'Fresh from the Congo, ladies and gentlemen. For years they defied the might of the Belgian army and the blandishments of the emissaries of Christ. They are cannibals. Only now am I weaning them away from human flesh'.

A youth at my side leaned forward and touched the foot of the nearest cannibal. 'Hey, Charlie', he said. 'What picture is on at the Tivoli tonight'?

Cowboy', said Charlie. 'Seen it before. Hang on a bit, Ern. This cannibal lark knocks off in about an hour. Hold my spear while I nip off and have a word with my Uncle Jack over there'. And off he hopped, with the barker calling him back angrily to the Limpopo.

Culturally Barry has worn its hat with a swagger. For all the years I lived there the shelves of its public library provided me with a matchless feast. Whoever built the collection had the whole human mind in view, and that is an article that keeps its head well down and is hard to present in full. It is a place full of charm and insight and among its shelves, not merely on the written page but in real life, I met many sweetly serene sages who led me into every corner of Barry's richly flavoured artistic life. Talents of the highest kind have acted, sung, danced and painted with lavish ease.

Of Barry's many fine schools I can talk of only one with intimate authority. The Barry Grammar School has been one of the most distinguished of its kind in Britain. You will find in every part of the world men who remember Dr Edgar Jones' Friday morning recitals of verse and music with deep affection. I have met the most arrant philistines who confess to having been touched by the magic of those communications of joy.

There was a sparkle of unique character about so many of the men and boys who made up the society of that school. D. J. P. Richards, the fanatical athlete, circling the field on a ten-mile training walk after school, his razor-thin body covered only by a flimsy, bikini-type pair of shorts. A woman on the top deck of a passing bus stared at him in drop-jawed disbelief, 'Oh, God, it's Gandhi'.

There was David Walters, who succeeded Tom Davies as Deputy Head. He lived in a reverie of regret for the fields and streams of Cardiganshire. He taught Chemistry and hated it. I found him once in the staff-room making a primitive sort of broom with twigs and a length of wire. He asked me, 'Can you make one of these, Thomas?' 'No'. 'Well, you'd better learn'. He made a gesture that took in the whole school. 'These places are not going to last for ever, you know'.

One sorts through the remembered faces with relish. John Lennox, Liberal orator of remarkable force and man of inexhaustible goodness. Percy Fisher, image of English dignity and firmness, as fine a centurion of the academic legion as ever held the line against ignorance and bad manners. Howard Francis, connoisseur of contemporary writing and for long a dynamo of the Barry Arts Society. George Young Smith, war-stricken and indomitable apostle of cricket, High Toryism and mathematics, marshalling his serfs for a stint on the heavy roller as implacably as Pharaoh enrolled the Israelites to break their backs on the pyramids.

Reginald Mills, spirit of singing joy as multi-literally creative as Michelangelo. J. J. Jones, whose mind banged on the bars of so many frustrations, his head clanked like a smithy. Teifion Phillips, the present Headmaster, with whom I discussed life nourishingly on countless homeward walks down Jenner Road and who trained as brilliant a body of young historians as this generation has known.

And over all the years the insistent relish of deep, hymnal harmonies struck morning after morning by Griffith Caradoc Hughes, Glyn Davies and Sidney Jones. With the draconian voice of E. T. Griffiths, Licensié of the Paris Sorbonne, storm-loving fugitive from the lowest peasantry, volcanic reformer and the school's third Head, reading out from the rostrum the names of malefactors bound for the detention-chamber, to bring us back into the unholy round and sound of reality.

Barry is a town uniquely of this age. Its people came there from all the counties of Britain, notably the South West. I choose a few at random. Tom Lewis, the immaculate and crotchetty ship-owner, who came here from Cardiff. He was a pioneer member of the Royal Flying Corps, a lover of law-suits, a hater of glasses with handles who ordered his beer two pints at a time. He had a watch fitted with so many complex devices it did everything except offer itself in marriage. He came to live on a certain spot on a Barry hillside because a con-sortium of doctors had told him it was an area where the average life-expectancy was the highest in Britain.

Ella Baldwin Smith, Headmistress, Esperantist, who came from the same village as the Brontë sisters and was once threatened with gaol in Berlin for leading a deputation to the Kaiser in 1912 demanding peace and an end to helmets and spiked moustaches.

Albert Bugler, immovably loyal trade-unionist, grower of champion onions, proponent of swingeingly radical opinions. He was in the trenches of Flanders at the age of 16. His mother kept a lodging-house for the navvies who built Barry Docks, and his father had a business selling coke. Each morning, as he made ready to go down to the dockside for his coke, he would hide Albert among the wet sacks to be counted as part of the weight when they jolted over the weighbridge. On the return journey the boy frolicked alongside the loaded cart, winking sardonically at the weighbridge man as he continued to wink throughout his long and exuberantly useful life.

The town grows. Marine Drive, built on the very lip of Bull's Nose Cliff, edges towards the steps up and down which Jack Petersen toiled as he worked his way to a heavy-weight title-fight. The acres of Highlight Farm, home of the Lakins, now house a thickening suburb.

The interior of the totally transformed *Colc* *Arms* would not be instantly recognised by th thousands of the American advance-guard wh camped with their tanks along the Port Road i the Second World War. The town is now ac ministratively part of the Vale which has alway been its complement and reservoir.

To the west of Barry is a ring of villages ric in tranquillity and revered taverns. From some o them the Barry Grammar School drew its fines talent. Glyn Daniel, on his way to Cambridg and fame, made his start by uncovering tessellated Roman pavement at Llantwit. Keit Thomas, of Pancross Farm, Llancarfan, ha thrown powerful new beams of light on th darker sides of the 17th century.

Ideally every town school should have a high proportion of boys and girls from villages. I broadens the spectrum of awareness within the school. But Barry had another advantage in this connection. It was an ocean-going place, the least parochial place I have ever come across. It is a town that has always taken easily and well to strangers. It was created by a world on the move and all the earth's continents were its familiars. The boom of lightships and the whistle blasts of passing freighters are in its speech. It still tingles with the shock of its beginnings.

RURAL BARRY

In 1881 the 'beautiful little country village of Barry', smaller and more compact than Cadoxton, had a population of 85 living in some 17 dwellings. These were Barry House—the residence of Colonel Romilly, the Lord of the Manor—a few scattered cottages, the village shop (now 6 St Nicholas Road), some farmhouses and the quaintly thatched *Ship Inn* much used for summer picnics. In addition there were the 13th century ruins of Barry Castle and the parish church dedicated to St Nicholas. The latter was rebuilt 1874-76 on the site of an ancient whitewashed church which had been a famous landmark for sailors in the Bristol Channel. The Old Harbour, a tidal estuary separating Barry Island from the mainland, had been involved in coastal trade from the late 13th century and was in use until *c.*1900

2   This photograph of the *Ship Hotel c.*1885 formerly hung in the foyer of the present hotel erected in the summer of 1891 on the site of the thatched inn. The George family who kept the inn probably appear in the photograph. They are buried in the churchyard of the former parish church dedicated to St Nicholas

3 Old Village, Barry, in 1898. 'Jordan's Cottage' with its thatched roof and rustic porch is in the foreground. The cottage and stile have been demolished

4 Old Village *c*.1905. The row of labourers' cottages (right) and 'Jordan's Cottage' (extreme left) were built *c*.1857/1861 by the Romilly Estate. Rose Cottage which lies between them was Green House Farm in 1622. The Barry Preservation Society has been successful in preserving the remaining cottages

5 Castle Farm *c.*1896, was reputedly built in the 16th century with stones from the ruins of Barry Castle. It was destroyed by fire in February 1912. The farmer, Charles Morgan (d.1927), could remember the time when the postman announced his arrival in the village by blowing a horn

6 Barry Castle, 1898. The 13th century gateway and portcullis chamber still survive. The de Barri family probably erected the castle which has a fine view of the Old Harbour and Bristol Channel

7/8 Before the construction of the docks the paths of East Barry House, a residence in its own grounds, went uninterruptedly down to the edge of a small tidal inlet. The house is demolished and Barclays Bank is built on the site. It is believed to have stood on the site of the medieval manor house of East Barry which in the 15th century belonged to the Andrews family who later resided at Cadoxton Court. The photographs were taken *c*.1884

CADOXTON OLD VILLAGE

A century ago the village of Cadoxton with its 'charming little cottages radiant in the splendour of their annual coat of whitewash' and the ancient parish church of St Cadoc's was a quiet and attractive place. One visitor wrote in the *Cardiff and Merthyr Guardian* 31 May 1862, 'The church and part of the village stand in a small deep valley—a beautiful spot wherein to worship God, far from the busy hum of the world and all its turmoil'. The majority of the 303 inhabitants of 1881 were Welsh speaking and lived off the land. The religious needs of the people were provided for by the whitewashed parish church and four chapels—Philadelphia Baptist (1813), Bethel (Welsh) Wesleyan (1815), Sion Calvinistic Methodist (1815) and the English Wesleyan (1862). The nucleated village was the centre for surrounding farmers and consisted of a general store-cum-post office, a blacksmith shop and carpenters' premises and the 'New Mill' powered by water on Cadoxton Moor. The social needs of the villagers were centred on the three quaint old inns, the *Three Bells, Wenvoe Arms, King William IV*—and the Old Elm Tree which acted as the focal point of the village

9 The Old Elm Tree at the foot of Pencoedtre Hill was a familiar landmark. The retaining wall was placed around it during its later years. Many protested at the removal of the dead tree in the summer of 1899. Behind it is the old Knap House demolished 1910

10 The Old Elm Tree and Knap House in the early 1890s showing the tree before its retaining wall was built. The artist, John Clark Fairbairn (d.1913), the grandson of a Midlothian farmer, came to Barry in 1889 where he set up as a newsagent and tobacconist at 55 Vere Street, Cadoxton

11 This view from Hatch Hill shows the village west of Brock Street, about 1910. The road running down the hill is narrow and unmetalled; the hump-back bridge gave the road its name—Bridge Street. The nearby ruins are those of Hatch Farm

CADOXTON

12 The old village has changed little during the present century. Oddfellows' House on the corner of Brock Street and Cowbridge Street, demolished *c*.1932, was the site of a school in 1791 which had an annual examination

13 The National School, Cadoxton, opened in 1847, was built on part of a garden given by the Rev Gabriel Powell, the rector, 'for the education of poor children in the parishes of Cadoxton and Merthyrdovan and as a residence for the Schoolmaster'

14 The snow covered church in *c*.1906 joins with the previous picture to give a panoramic view of the village. A horse-drawn landau is waiting at the church gate

15 William Edward Brock and Ada Louisa Jenkins members of old and respected families were married on 15 September 1909 at St Cadoc's. Children on the bank opposite the church are chanting for loose change to be thrown, an ancient practice which continued until the early 1950s

16 Mrs Cutter and a child are near the gate of Rock Cottage. Standing by the wooden barrel in the Coldbrook stream is William Spickett. With his brother David he conveyed coal for sale about Cadoxton in a wheel-barrow, at 1s. 3d. per cwt. best quality

17 'Bryn Teg' and 'Bryn Glas' on top of Little Hill, Cadoxton Common, prior to exploitation of the hill by the District quarrymen at the turn of the century. The houses in the foreground are 'Rock Cottage' and Oddfellows' House

18 Weston Farm was demolished *c*.1902 in connection with work on the construction of the lower portion of Gladstone Road. At high tide, water covered Weston Moor and came up to the farm wall shown in the photograph. To the left of the farm is the Navvy Mission

19 St Cadoc's has long been a popular venue for the solemnisation of weddings. In this picture *c*.1910 three landaus with drivers wearing button holes can be seen outside the church. Note the white covers on the horses ears signifying a marriage. Black covers were worn at funerals

THE TOWN

No place in Wales developed so rapidly in transition from village to town as Barry at the turn of the century. The construction of docks destroyed overnight the seclusion and rural charm of the villages of Barry, Merthyr Dyfan and Cadoxton which in 1896 were joined to form the civil parish of Barry. Immigrants from the rest of Wales, the West Country, Ireland, Scotland and elsewhere flooded into the area to find work. Within 40 years the population grew from 500 in 1881 to 38,945 in 1921. Since that date the increase has been relatively small, the census for 1971 being 41,578. By the outbreak of the Great War, Barry had grown into a town of nearly two hundred streets. It was mostly well paved, well lighted and with a good supply of gas and clean water. The main roads and shopping centres had emerged and most of them are illustrated

20 The old lane leading to Holton Farm, situated near the present Theatre Royal, became in the 1890s Holton Road, one of Barry's main thoroughfares and shopping centres. This view, late autumn c.1909, was taken from King Square looking westwards

21 Holton Road *c*.1910 looking west between its junction with Richard Street and Evans Street. The shop signs, sun awnings, gas lamps and unmetalled road make this a typical early 20th century view

22 Holton Road in the early 1920s looking west with the turning to Richard Street on the right. On the left can be seen the shop of A. H. Buckland, clothier, and Oliver's Shoe Shop

23 Holton Road *c.*1910 looking eastwards to King Square. The turning to Lombard Street is on the near left. On the right is B. Stone, picture frame maker, and Lawrence the pawnbroker. The London 1/6d Bazaar is on the corner with Thompson Street

24 Holton Road in 1930. Left is the Amy Evans Hospital. A child is standing near the junction with Watson Street on the corner of which is the quaint Victorian edifice 'The Towers'. St Mary's Church is farther down the road

HOLTON ROAD AND ST MARY'S CHURCH, BARRY.

25 Wyndham Street *c*.1910. The Barry General Accident and Surgical Hospital opened in September 1908. The former Welsh Methodist Church in Tynewydd Road is now the 'New Jerusalem' Congregational Church

26 Court Road at its junction with Holton Road in 1930. The Fire Engine Station, opened in 1901, is to be replaced by a new station on Port Road scheduled to open in September 1977. Holton Road School (right) opened in 1892

COURT ROAD FIRE STATION AND SCHOOL, BARRY DOCK.

27 Early Broad Street *c.*1885 (named Barry Dock Road until 1899) was made of temporary wooden buildings with brick chimneys. The shop nearest is advertising earthenware. Further along a sign advertises 'Evans & Co. Grocers'

28 Broad Street *c.*1914 looking west from Priory Hill to the Barry Hotel. The junction with Island Road is on the left. A disastrous fire in 1923 gutted the ornate brick façade of the Barry & District Co-operative Society premises behind the delivery van

29 Children playing in the snow at the lower end of Park Crescent. The tower belongs to Bethel English Baptist Chapel erected in 1903 in Harbour Road. The absence of All Saints Church built in 1908 helps date this picture

30 Vere Street *c*.1914 looking towards Weston Square. In the early 1890s before the emergence of Holton Road it housed the council and newspaper offices. At its junction with Harvey Street (right) is the Cadoxton Picture Palace which opened in 1914

31 Harvey Street *c*.1905 showing the limestone and yellow brick built houses in the older part of the town. Beyond its crossing with Quarella Street is the tree-lined rise of Kenilworth Road. An early type of baby carriage is coming round the corner from Moxon Street

32 Barry Road *c*.1910 looking west to tower of the refuse destructor built 1901 (demolished 1971). On the right is C. H. Lewis' horse-drawn bakery van. His father came from Stoke in 1888 to Palmerstown where he ran a bakery and grocery business before moving to Barry Road in 1893

33 Sea View Terrace prior to the construction of Victoria Park wall in 1907. Thomas Ewbank had the ivy clad 'Pen-y-Bryn' built with Shap granite from his birthplace in Westmorland. It was later the home of Christopher Howe, assistant overseer of the parish and veteran of the American Civil War

34 Weston Hill *c*.1910. The former iron building served as a Congregational Church. On the horizon is Sea View Terrace. To the right of it is the 'Mount' which in this and the previous picture had a thatched roof

35 Cadoxton House was the residence of Dr Edward Treharne (d.1905) before John Jewel Williams, the builder (d.1912), a veteran of the Siege of Sebastopol resided there. Jewel Williams, who came from North Devon, also built the *Royal Hotel* and Jewel Street. Old Mill Farm, partly of 17th century date and the oldest occupied house in Cadoxton, is shown with a thatched roof

BARRY ISLAND AND COLD KNAP

Before the construction of the docks Barry Island could only be approached at low tide by steppin[g] stones across the Cadoxton River. There were only two houses. One was a ruined farmhouse whic[h] earlier in the century had belonged to John Thomas, a great eccentric who augmented his living b[y] selling rabbits to passing ships. He had made his money from the wreck of the *Frolic*. A strong swimmer he would cross over to the Island when the tide was full by putting his valuables in his top hat an[d] hanging on to his horse's tail. The remaining building, the old *Marine Hotel*, said to be partly buil[t] from wrecks, was a 'country refreshment house' mostly used by picnic parties. It had been built in 185[?] by Francis Crawshay as a summer residence. In May 1879 the Island was closed to visitors by its owner Lord Windsor, and converted into a rabbit warren. Five years later the construction of docks had th[e] effect of joining the Island to the mainland and destroying forever its seclusion so that in August 1891 [a] visitor to Whitmore Bay was able to write 'Already the sands are studded with bathing machines an[d] Barry bids fair to be a favourite seaside resort'

36 The Switchback Railway from the London Exhibition was a big attraction at Barry Island prior to the Great War. On the extreme right people are walking along the 'Half-penny' promenade. The old pavilion of the Barry Athletic Club is on the left

37 The entrance to the Switchback Railway was located to the west of the Gents cloakroom in Paget Road. The Parade, the tide in the old harbour, and an undeveloped district now occupied by Lakeside and Marine Drive can also be seen

38 The Figure 8 Railway, Barry Island, was built in 1912. It was replaced in 1939 when the Scenic Railway (demolished 1973) was erected on the same site

39 The Midget Motors opened on Collins' Fairground in 1927. The different colour cars were driven by two 12 volt batteries and could carry two for a 6d. ride twice around the track which measured 150′ × 50′. Pictured in back row (left to right) are Mr Winchester, manager, Nic Walls, track foreman, and Miss Flossie Williams, cashier

40 Beach donkeys have always been popular with children and no more so than in this picture dated *c.* 1905

THE DONKEYS ON THE SANDS, BARRY ISLAND.

The 'Half-penny' promenade, so ...ed as this was the entrance fee (pay-...e at turn-stiles either end), ran along ...top of sand dunes skirting the length ...Whitmore Bay. It was made more ...active by two bridges built over ...tunnels giving access to the sand

The Barry Urban Authority, with ...vernment financial aid to ease un-...ployment, began building the sea wall ...d promenade in 1922. Previously a low ...ll surmounted by iron railings separated ...e dunes from the beach. At full tide ...e stalls and pierrot tents made the beach very crowded

3 The Barry Urban Authority offered ...paces to let each year by public auction ...or the erection of stalls, roundabouts ...nd swings. The construction of the sea ...vall and promenade ended this practice in 1923

44/45   Treharne Pier in the late 1890s. A small wooden pier, it ran from Treharne Point (now Friar's Point) into Whitmore Bay. Its name was derived from a former owner of the island. The pier was erected in 1858 by Francis Crawshay, the ironmaster, for the use of the yacht he built on the island. The yacht became famous in English Channel ports because of the eccentricities of the 'Old Welshman' who paid his crew double wages and all hands were piped for grog twice a day. Whitmore, seen in the background, is scarcely developed. In 1902 the pier was demolished as unsafe

46 Friar's Point House was built as the *Marine Hotel* in 1858 by Francis Crawshay for use by his guests. Crawshay had a great liking for the sea and the house had sleeping berths like those on a ship. It became a private residence *c*.1900, and was renovated and considerably enlarged by Sir William Graham

47 The sea wall and promenade in the late 1920s. Plans were approved in 1910 but development was delayed by the Great War and work on the scheme did not commence until 1922. Two rows of changing huts can be seen on the beach

48 Watchtower Bay in 1898. The Watch Tower, built *c*.1865, was used as a coastguard station until 1906. The thatched Cold Knap farm, the oldest occupied house in Barry, was once the residence of Richard Garby *c*.1765-1831 'a smuggler in a large way'. The dark arches belong to old limekilns

49 The Marine Boating Lake, Cold Knap *c*.1936. The lake is in the shape of a Welsh harp. Together with the Swimming Lido it was built in 1926 with financial help from the government to ease unemployment

50 The Shirvington family at a picnic party at Bendrick Beach in 1928. The black outline of Bendrick Rock is completely submerged when the tide is at full. A ship approaching Barry Docks is being met by a pilot cutter

SPORT, ENTERTAINMENT AND SPECIAL OCCASIONS

51 Barry Unionist football team, 1901. Two cockerels were raffled to equip the team which later won the Welsh Association Football Cup. Their pitch was at the Buttrills and goal-posts etc., had to be carried up there before a game could commence

52 Barry Shop Assistants A.F.C., 1908/1909 taken at the Buttrills. W. C. Braund, seated on the left, was the captain

53 Barry Romilly A.F.C., 1909/1910 at Romilly Park where they trained and played in the Cardiff and District League. In later years known as the 'Barry West End', their changing rooms were at Tom Trought's shop, 16 Broad Street. Two of the players later turned professional

54 The successful Pyke Street team which won the Barry and District School Shield, 1906/1907. Headmaster, Mr Williams, is on the left. Billy Saunders, captain, holding the ball, lived in Woodlands Road and later played for Barry Town

55 Cadoxton Schools A.F.C., 1911/1912. Headmaster, Mr Thomas Ewbank, stands on the left, and his deputy, Mr A. W. Storey, is on the right

56 Cadoxton Wesleyan Church A.F.C. winners of the Bon Accord Cup; Champions S.S. Section, Barry League, for 1922/23 season. In this picture the captain, R. Sheppard, is holding the ball. W. J. Cousins, the ironmonger, is on the right

57 Barry A.F.C., 1920/21. In the back row are E. Beresford, trainer (first left), Councillor C. B. Griffiths, chairman (centre), and S. Beaumont, manager (extreme right). Bob John (second right, front row) later played for Arsenal and Wales

58 Barry R.F.C., 1913/14 at Romilly Park, where they played and trained. On the left of the captain, T. Howell (holding the ball), is W. M. Douglas (President), who won Senior Welsh caps while playing for Cardiff in 1886/87. Two of his sons are in the front row and one of them is wearing his father's cap

59 Barry R.F.C., 1919/20 outside the *Ship Hotel*. The players in green and white jerseys were captained by C. Harris (with the ball). Councillor W. Gameson (Chairman), standing on right, was a former professional Rugby League player who helped keep rugby alive in Barry in the difficult days after the Great War

60 Barry Parade R.F.C., 1911/12 at Romilly Park. W. M. Douglas (in centre wearing a cap) was club chairman. The team was the ancestor of the Barry Rugby Team which in the 1920s was still sometimes called the Barry Romilly Rugby Club or Barry Paraders

61 Barry County School 1st XV, 1927/28. R. W. Boon, captain (holding ball), was the first Barry-born player to receive a rugby international senior cap in 1930 and went on to be capped 16 times by Wales. A. J. Risman (third left, back row) ranks as one of the greatest Rugby League players ever

62 A match is in progress in this photograph of Romilly Park Bowling Club in August 1916. At this date not all the land facing the Park had been developed for housing. St Osyth, the large Victorian Gothic house on the right, has been demolished and replaced by flats

63 Barry Athletic Bowling Club, 1919 season. W. H. Baker, the captain, seated in the middle on the bench, was manager of the Romilly Hall cinema. Seated on the ground, bottom right, is Percy Holloway (Vice-Capt.), a Welsh bowls champion who represented Wales in the 1934 Commonwealth Games

64 Cadoxton Bowling Club, 1916. The Club opened in 1908 shortly before its great rival at Romilly Park. Councillor David Lloyd (President), a founder-member, is seen, sixth from right in the middle row, and J. Felix Williams, Junior, a Welsh International Bowler, is the young man in the middle of the front row

65 Barry Cricket and Athletic Club, 1913, standing in front of the pavilion. W. D. John (Captain) is seated in centre of front row. Frank Pinch (third from left, back row) played for Glamorgan during the inter-war years

66 St Aidan's Gymnastic Club, 1923. The club which was attached to St Aidan's Church, Main Street, Cadoxton from 1921 to 1960 won a national and international reputation with men like W. Buffin (Hon. Instructor), standing on right, and Jimmy Gimlett, seated second from left

67 Central Park at the rear of the Library and Council Offices was laid out on the site of an old quarry. Although only 1¼ acres in extent it has always been highly appreciated by the inhabitants of the town centre

68 Barry Yacht and Motor Boat Club Regatta Committee, 1930. Rear Commodore W. Chalmers is holding the silver top cane. To his left are Commodore N. Bate and E. C. Wood, Chairman. The club, which has its headquarters next to the Lifeboat Station, was founded in 1927 and celebrates its 50th anniversary this year

69 Barry Town Band, 1911. Charles Dunkley, the conductor, is on the ground to right of the drum. Arthur Pepworth, the drummer, is on the other side of him. The first brass band, formed at Cadoxton in 1888, was involved in festivities at the opening of the dock

70 Barry Silver Prize Band at Central Park, 1925. It was just before this that the band changed its name from the Barry Red Cross Band. It disbanded in 1959 to be succeeded in 1974 by the present Vale of Glamorgan Brass Band

71 Romilly School Choir on their return from Colwyn Bay National Eisteddfod 1910, where they kept an audience of 12,000 spellbound to win first prize. Under the baton of their legendary conductor W. M. Williams, father of Grace Williams the composer, they won a world-wide reputation

72 Romilly School Choir on their North America tour of 1914, standing on the steps of the Y.M.C.A. in Toronto. They were given a warm welcome by Welsh Americans and they sang for President Wilson at the White House where each boy received a five dollar bill from the President

73 Barry Male Voice Choir, *c.*1906 outside the Institute, Woodlands Road, with D. J. Thomas their first conductor (1902-1941). The choir was formed in February 1902 and was composed of about 12 young men of Tynewydd Congregational Church who called themselves the Barry Dock Glee Party

74 May 24, 1900, was observed as a general holiday in honour of Queen Victoria's birthday and as a celebration of the relief of Mafeking. Some 10,000 witnessed a grand display of fireworks on Barry Island and the roasting of this ox which was cut up and distributed to the town's poor

75 *Opposite:* The King Edward VII Coronation bonfire was lit on Friar's Point, Monday night, 30 Ju 1902, in the presence of the Council chairman and hundreds of townspeople. The fire which burnt faultless was seen throughout the Barry district and was distinctly visible from the Somerset and Devon coast

CORONATION ✦ BONFIRE,

BARRY ISLAND,

FIRED JUNE 30th, 1902.

Centre Pole, 55 feet.   Circumference, 120 feet.   Height, 45 feet.   Weight, 185 tons.

T. L. HOWE

Penarth & Barry

76 The cross in St Cadoc's Churchyard was erected on the restored medieval calvary steps as a Great War Memorial. Made of blue Forest of Dean stone it is a copy of one at Bonvilston. On Sunday afternoon 12 November 1922 two to three thousand people filled the church and churchyard to overflowing when in an impressive ceremony the cross was unveiled by Col. Hybart who led the first unit of local men who left with the 1914 Expeditionary Force in France. The Bishop of Llandaff solemnly dedicated the cross 'To the Glory of God and in loving memory of the 109 brave men of Cadoxton Barry who fell in the Great War 1914-

77 Twenty thousand people gathered on Saturday 20 May 1910 to hear W. R. Lee, J.P., chairman of the Urban Authority, read out the Royal Proclamation of King George V. This was followed by a 21 gun salute in a field at the top of Tynewydd Road

78 The bandstand at Victoria Park, Cadoxton (now demolished) was a popular venue for open air concerts. Wounded soldiers, wearing their distinctive blue and grey uniforms, are escorted by Red Cross nurses at a function during the Great War

79 Recruiting sergeants head a band and a detachment of soldiers marching up Main Street in a recruiting drive during the early pre-conscription days of the Great War

80 The first contingent of U.S.A. troops to land in Britain during the Great War disembarked at Barry Docks and marched to King Square on 31 July 1918 where they were given an official reception. Led by Col. Mortimer they were part of a force of 50,000 American Troops destined for France

81 Dai Lossin's Cwm Scwt Invincibles played Dai Pepper's Cwmcoch Irresistibles on 2 May 1914 at Jenner Park before about 6,000 spectators. The famous comedian George Formby, Senior, consented to kick off and proceeds were in aid of the St John Ambulance Brigade

TRADE

82 J. C. Meggitt established his timber importing business in 1884 and the first cargo was unloaded in the Old Harbour before the docks were ready. He was joined in 1888 by his brother-in-law, Sibbering Jones. In this picture, taken *c*.1900, are two of the horses in a fleet of 20 to 30 horses and wagons used during busy periods

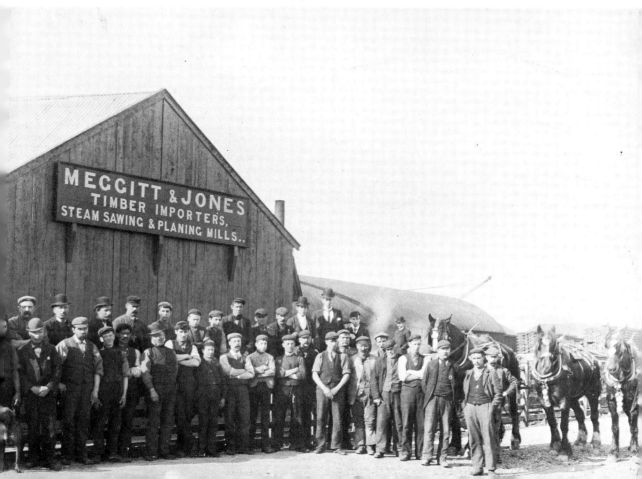

83 B. A. Walker's bread van in Broa
Street, 1908. He had established h
bakery at 264 Holton Road by 189
where he continued until the end of th
Great War when Ben Ashton took ove
the business. Half the bread round wa
taken over by E. A. Luxton, maste
baker, the author's grandfather

84 J. Rank Ltd., Atlantic Flour Mills, opened on the south side of Dock No. 2 in June 1905 to take full advantage of a dockside location. This picture, taken while men are still tiling the roof, shows a three masted barque unloading her cargo of grain

85 Thomas Evans (d.1902), a native of Cadoxton, lies buried in St Cadoc's churchyard, a short distance from the smithy which he kept and which this photograph depicts

86 Edward Evans (son of Thomas Evans), shoeing smith (first on the right), with workmen opposite his blacksmith's shop at the rear of 1 Brock Street, *c*.1900. Behind them are the garden wall and pine end of Golden Grove. Council workmen are with Mr Paulett's horse and cart used for refuse collection

87 General view of Thompson Street looking towards junction with Holton Road. The street was named after Thomas Roe Thompson (d.1919) a native of Sunderland who was a director of the Barry Dock and Railway Company. Demolished 1972, its heyday was prior to the Great War

88 Owen Jones, a native of Prestatyn, first set up business in Barry in 1889. The picture, taken in 1904, shows him standing outside his grocery and provision store at 45 Thompson Street

89 Harry Press of Frome, Somerset, established his fishmongers', fruiterers' and greengrocers' business at 176 Holton Road in 1902. This picture, taken *c.*1903, shows Mr Press wearing a 'Billinsgate straw' with his wife, dressed in black, and two assistants

90 In 1904 Mr Press moved to 93 Holton Road and in this picture taken at that time he is seen in front of the shop (holding the long arm) with his wife and an assistant. The business continues with his son Harry Press, Junior

91 Dan Evans, born on a farm in Llangadog, Carmarthenshire, opened an ironmongers' shop at 81 Holton Road in 1902 for W. H. Hooper. In 1905 he bought the shop and is the young man of 22 in the centre of picture. The business expanded until at his demise in 1972 it had 240 employees

92 W. J. Cousins, born in Blagdon Hill, Somerset, came to Barry at the turn of the century where he worked for J. H. Abbot, ironmonger, Holton Road, until in 1903 he established his ironmongers' business at 79 Main Street. In this picture of 1914 we see his four children

93 John Jones, a farmer's son from near St Clears, Carmarthenshire, set up his drapery business in Main Street, Cadoxton, in 1891. In 1900 he moved to Holton Road where in course of time three shops were opened. His son Mr Stewart Jones is on the right of this picture *c*.1914

94 John Lewis who came to Barry from Penarth is seen *c*.1906 standing in the doorway of his drapery business at 124 Holton Road. The other gentlemen are his brothers and by 1914 they were trading under the name of Lewis Brothers

95 Franz Joseph Greener left his native Bubenbach in the Black Forest, Germany, to avoid conscription by Bismarck. He opened a silversmiths' shop at Cadoxton in 1887 before moving in 1890 to 118 Holton Road where he is pictured *c*.1904 with two of his sons, Gabriel William (left) and Lawrence

96 Thomas Trought moved from 34 Glebe Street, Penarth, to run this confectionery shop at 16 Broad Street in 1903. In this *c*.1904 photograph the group standing in the doorway are, from left to right, Tom Trought, Polly Hill, shop assistant, Beatrice Irene Trought, Hannah Rachel Trought and Charles Carless

97 Jabez Malpas, who came from Chepstow, established his market garden business in Barry before the Great War and ran a greengrocery at 74 High Street. This c.1916 picture shows the delivery car inside the Harbour Road Nurseries with Lois and Agnes, his daughters, Fred Wall and Mrs Davies

98 Barry Garage, built in 1907. One of the first garages for motor repairs, it was on the corner of Broad Street and Flora Street (now College Road). The Barry Garage and Engineering works was run by Thomas White, later head of one of the largest private bus companies in the area

99 Barry Master Bakers' and Millers' Association on an annual outing in the early 1900s to Cheddar Gorge

100 The *Barry Herald* newspaper was published between 1896 and 1962. Its office at 31 Holton Road on the corner with Lombard Street is now Decoflair Ltd., wallpaper and paint discount store

101 The Parade Cafe in the Parade *c.*1930 also provided groceries and provisions. It is now the American Graffiti

102 John Lewis Davies of Llanon, Cardigan, chairman of the Urban Authority in 1901, established his corn store in Vere Street by 1890 and continued there until 1914 when A. L. Davie, one of his four sons, took over the business. Another son, Ernest Ivor Davies, Medical Officer of Health for Barry (1935-1947), is pictured c.1904 in the doorway with 'Joe' the family terrier and rat catcher

103 Stanley Yeandle came from Wiveliscombe, Somerset, in the autumn of 1919 and opened his butchers' shop at 19 Dunraven Street by the spring of 1921. In this picture, taken Christmas 1925, Stanley Yeandle is on the left and his son John, the present proprietor, is in the doorway holding a longarm

104 Fred Robinson began his business as a haulier collecting seamen's bags off ships until he won the contract to deliver parcels for Barry Dock station. His son Walter is seen on the right before setting off to the Barry Horse and Flower Show *c*.1912/13. The *Castle Hotel* and Morgan Street are in the background

105 Many businessmen had their own delivery service. This delivery cart, belonging to Harry Press, is seen in Hayes Road, Sully, *c*.1914

RELIGION, EDUCATION
AND PUBLIC SERVICES

106   St Cadoc's Church c.1900. The present southern boundary wall built with stones from the demolished Weston Farm extended the churchyard and replaced the tumbledown wall pictured here. Cowbridge Street had not yet been cut and low limestone walls divided the land into allotments and orchards

107 St Cadoc's prior to the restoration of the nave and lower part of tower in 1885. The church was closed that summer and marriages solemnised at St Andrews. Frescoes discovered in the nave were destroyed when the walls collapsed. The nave and porch are whitewashed and there is a thatched roof on the *Three Bells*

108 Handsome wreaths were laid at the base of the memorial cross at the close of the dedication while the congregation sang the hymn 'Lest we Forget'. Comparison with the previous plate will show the exterior changes made by the 1885 restoration

109 The rapid growth of Barry led to the building of many new churches. On 21 October 1903 Mrs Laura Jenner, Wenvoe Castle, a patron of the living of Cadoxton, laid the foundation stone for the church of St Mary in Holton Road. It was dedicated by Bishop Pritchard-Hughes on 22 June 1905

110 The Theatre Royal and Palace of Varieties in Iddesleigh Street, Cadoxton, built in 1891 was the first permanent theatre in Barry. Both the street and building changed their names. Iddesleigh Street was absorbed in Main Street and the bankrupt theatre, licensed for divine service, was dedicated to St Aidan, 2 February 1910

111 Merthyr Dyfan church *c*.1905. Dedicated to Saints Dyfan and Teilo, the church is a small edifice consisting of a 13th century chancel and nave, a south porch, and western embattled Tudor tower with three bells. The fields are now occupied by the Colcot housing estate

112 St Paul's, the daughter church of St Dyfan and Teilo, was consecrated in 1893. This picture shows members of the church at a social function *c*.1900

Cadoxton Wesleyan Church. 1863.

113 The English Wesleyan Ch[...]
opened for public worship in Oc[...]
1862, was built on the north we[...]
edge of Cadoxton Common. It is p[...]
larly supposed that a box conta[...]
coins and newspapers of the period
placed in the foundations. This pictu[...]
prior to the addition of transepts in [...]

114 Members of Cadoxton Wesleyan Methodist church *c.*1898 on an outing to Garth Mountain. They travelled by train from Cadoxton to Creigiau. The church minister at this time was the Rev. James H. Watson

115 John Thomas, deacon and Sunday School teacher at Seion Welsh Calvinistic Methodist chapel, Pontypridd Street, is surrounded by his Sunday School class on an outing *c.*1908. The chapel is demolished and houses have been built on the site

116 A pageant put on by Barry churches was held in the Theatre Royal about 1916. In this picture is seen the entry from St Paul's Church. The 'boy bishop' is Mr R. Limebear of Queen Street

117 Members of the Church of Christ standing outside their Meeting House in 1905. The church, called the Christian's Meeting House, was still functioning in 1926 but of recent years it has been used by Mr Cowie for his upholstery business

118 The boys of Cadoxton School marshalled on the Common 1898 for barbell and flag drill with the School drum and Fife Band which performed at social functions prior to the Great War. The thatched 'Pleasant View' is demolished

119 The first board school in Barry, built on Cadoxton Common in 1879, was greatly extended with the influx of people into the new town. Thomas Ewbank, headmaster 1879-1921, is standing fifth from left, back row, in this picture of the school staff in 1896

120 To relieve congestion in the schools at Barry Dock the Urban Authority erected this handsome block of schools in Gladstone Road in 1906. This picture was taken shortly after the school's opening and prior to the setting out of Gladstone Gardens

121 The schoolmaster (on right) is supervising boys in flag drill practice in the front yard of Cadoxton School c.1910

122 The County Intermediate School at the Buttrills opened on 1 October 1896. It was co-educational until the autumn of 1913 when the girls moved to their own grammar school nearby. In this picture of the staff of the Dual School 1912-13 Major Edgar Jones is in the centre of the middle row

123 Staff of the Boys' County School, 1933. Major Edgar Jones, headmaster 1899-1933 in the middle of the front row, is one of the most illustrious names in Welsh educational history

124 Staff of High Street School, 1921. In the front row are Harry Whitehouse, Headmaster (middle), D. J. Thomas (left), and Evan Powell (fourth left), the conductor and deputy conductor of the Barry Male Voice. E. G. Habbakuk, second from left back row, is the father of Sir Hrothgar Habbakuk, Vice-Chancellor of Oxford University and Principal of Jesus College, a Welsh foundation

125 This picture will bring back memories for some of the older people in the town. Loaned by Reg. East of 5 Windsor Road (fourth left, back row) it is of Standard 1V High Street Boys' School in 1921. The class teacher on the right was Alfred Morgan

126   A class outside Holton Road Girls' School in 1921

127   Form two of Palmerstown Road Infants School c.1906. Some of the children are holding toys. The
teacher, Miss Roberts (top right), who lived in Gladstone Road, is holding a baby sister in her arms

128 Sea View Labour Club, Dock View Road, was used as a hospital in the Great War. This picture taken inside a ward shows Red Cross nurses and wounded soldiers seated by their beds. Behind them on the wall can be seen their temperature charts

129 A tableau included in the first schools' concert held at the Romilly Hall about 1899 or 1900. The young red cross nurses, stretcher bearers and patients were pupils of Hannah Street School

130 On Wednesday 22 April 1908 Councillor W. J. Williams J.P., Chairman of the Barry Urban Authority, unlocked the outer door of the new Public Offices, King Square, with a handsome gold key presented to him by the architects. Members of the council are pictured outside their new office

131 These four ladies (left to right) Mrs Humphreys, Robins Lane, Mrs Bishop, Main Street, Mrs Syms, Barry Road, and Mrs Mary Ann Ashton, Robins Lane, attended a party given by the Urban Authority at Gladstone Road School on Friday 1 January 1909 to commemorate the start of the State Pension scheme

132 The Barry G.P.O. staff 1893 in front of their headquarters, wooden buildings sited on waste ground facing the *Barry Dock Hotel.* Postmen walked 20 miles a day for wages between 17/- and 24/- a week. Duty commenced at 5.30 a.m. and ended at approximately 6.00 p.m. Ivor Day (second left, middle row) is the father of Ivor R. Day, B.E.M., of Pontypridd Road, Barry

133 This Merryweather, the first motor fire engine in Barry, was purchased in May 1913. The machine, painted vermillion with the words 'Barry Fire Brigade' written on each side in gold letters, is pictured with its crew outside the County School where it fought a fire in September 1913

134 Barry Fire Brigade in front of the Public Offices 1921. The Merryweather engine stayed in service until February 1940 when replaced by a new Dennis enclosed appliance. It was kept as a reserve in World War II and sold for scrap in August 1944

135 Ivor Turner was a founder member of the Woodpeckers, the first patrol of Barry Scouts in 1908. He was the first King's Scout and first Silver Wolf in Barry

136 Edward Davies, a sergeant in the Boer War, came to Barry to help build the Theatre Royal. He was the first Scoutmaster of the First Barry Troop which grew out of the original Woodpecker patrol. Their headquarters were in the school-room attached to the Wesleyan Church, Porthkerry Road

137 Ivor Turner got his friends together to form the Woodpecker Patrol, acknowledged to be the first in the town but closely followed by a patrol in Cadoxton. The photograph was taken in September 1912 when Ivor Turner (centre, front row) was about to emigrate to Canada. Sid Luen (third right, front) is still a very active personality in Barry

138 The First Barry King's Troop with the King's Banner they won in 1911 and the two succeeding years. A handsome Union Jack with gold lettering, it had the Scout Badge in the centre with a crown above. It was presented by George V to the best Scout Troop in the country

COMMUNICATIONS

139 This view *c*.1905 from Palmerstown Road shows a G class Barry Locomotive pulling passenger coaches from Cadoxton Station along the Dinas Powis line. On the right of the smoke is the now demolished Welsh Wesleyan Chapel, Cadoxton Common (built 1815)

140 Cadoxton Station *c*.1905. The platforms were lit by electricity in 1902. Barry Locomotive 58 B1 Class built by the Vulcan Foundry in 1892 is at No. 2 Platform. Locomotive 94 J Class built by Sharp Stewart in 1899 is drawing in to No. 1 Platform. The Station was destroyed by fire in November 1914

VALE GLAMORGAN RAILWAY
PORTHKERRY VIADUCT
AUG 31ST 1896   AB

141 Porthkerry viaduct formed a vital link in the Vale of Glamorgan Railway between the collieries in the west and the agricultural districts of Bridgend and Barry. Construction started in 1894 but was not completed until July 1897, owing to difficulties in providing strong foundations. There were several collapses and one is clearly visible where a buckle can be seen in the pier on the right

142 The viaduct was opened for traffic on 1 December 1897 but was almost immediately closed again through the subsidence of the embankment and the third pier from the Barry end in the early hours of 10 January 1898

143   Railway Locomotive No. 143 the first of the L class built for Barry Railway Company by Hawthorn Leslie in 1914 is outside the Locomotive Running Sheds opposite Barry Station. Girl and boy cleaners were employed because during the Great War the Barry Railway released over 25% of its employees to the forces

144   By the Railways Act of 1921 the Barry Railway was amalgamated with the G.W.R. on 1 January 1922. Alf Mason, Station Master, Barry, and his staff are pictured at the time of amalgamation. Of the 148 Barry engines taken over 26 survived to British Railways in 1948

Council Offices & Library, Barry Dock.

145 In 1910 there were 92 horse brakes and waggonettes licensed to ply for hire, the principal operator being David Paulett of Cadoxton with 13 vehicles. This *c.*1912 view shows a waggonette of George Gay with, just visible on the extreme left, one of the newly introduced motor buses

146 By 1921 the horse brakes had been run off the road by the motors. Two years later there were 60 motor buses licensed on the local service. Charges of 'racing' and 'hanging on' were common. Leading the queue here is Barry 'bus No. 3, then Thomas's Maudslay and Watt's Austin charabancs

147 The Pioneer Motor Co. Ltd., was formed in 1911 with Rufus A. Davies, the auctioneer, as secretary. This green and yellow Commer bus, seen at Whitmore Bay, was nicknamed the *Titanic* due to the slope of the body. It earned £20 in 1d and 2d fares between King Square and Barry Island on Whit Monday 1913

148 In July 1920 Rufus Davies, now as Barry Motors Ltd., started the first regular service to Cardiff with the *Scarlet Pimpernel* and *Duchess*. The fare was 2/3d from *Barry Hotel* where this picture was taken

149 The ex-London open top Leyland double-decker seen opposite the Romilly Hall was brought to Barry in 1919 for Mrs Clara Thomas, the founder of Thomas's Motors. The saloon was also an ex-London bus operated in Barry by 'The Boatmen', the Central Motor Co., Buttrills Road

150 A typical charabanc outing of the late '20s. The Daimler 28-seater was new to J. P. King of Barry in July 1920. Later Thomas's Motors had it modernised by fitting pneumatic tyres and electric lighting. Passengers were expected to assist in erecting the hood!

151 Late in 1925 a group of local bus owners formed the Barry Associated Motors. Known as the 'Big Ten' they opened up new routes in the town with a fleet of yellow Thornycroft 20 seat saloons seen here when new in April 1926. They were subsequently absorbed by White's Motors

152 This 1928 A.D.C. coach was the forerunner of today's coaches. It was owned by Reliance Motors, Barry, who ran on the joint Cardiff lower road service for over 30 years

153 In order to relieve unemployment in Barry during the 1920s the Government gave financial grants for various public schemes including road widening. The helter-skelter dominates this 1928 Paget Road picture with the Gilford bus of White's Motors returning to Barry Docks while, behind the first aid tent, Thomas's Vulcan waits at the Cardiff stand

154 Looking down Friar's Road the water-chute and Figure 8 can be seen on the right and between the two B.A.M. buses Esplanade Buildings under construction, later to house the roller-skating rink

155 The road past the station and around the showground was to be two way traffic for many years. By 1930 Pat Collins had taken over the main showground from White Bros. who moved opposite on to the Cosy Corner site

156 This *c*.1904 car which formerly belonged to King Edward VII is standing in front of 'Beaconsfield'
(next to Romilly Schools and now demolished)

157 Ford Model T van used by Percy Hill for delivering boiled sweets from his warehouse at Bassett Street
Drill Hall. It was repainted in this startling livery by Geo. Letts at Gay's Cross Street Garage *c*.1920. Ford
vans of this type were the first motor vehicles of many Barry companies

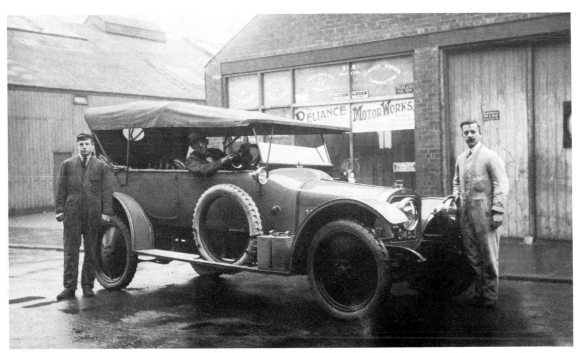

158 In 1919 the Reliance Motor Works was opened at 11 Holton Road by Messrs Shardelow and Andrews seen here with a sunbeam touring car. The garage was rebuilt after a serious fire in 1937 and was used as a bus garage by Reliance Motors and Red & White until 1956

159 'Dick' Bishop walked from his native Patchway, Bristol, to find work at Barry Dock. In the 1890s he set up as a butcher at 34 Vere Street. By 1906 he had moved to 81 Main Street and in this picture of the mid 1920s he is seen in the shop window on right. His son, Thomas, stands in the doorway behind his 1923 Rover motor cycle

THE DOCKS AND SHIPPING

Led by David Davies of Llandinam, Welsh colliery owners and ship owners built their own dock and rail facilities at Barry to meet a world wide demand for Welsh steam coal. Two docks were built between Barry Island and the mainland. Dock No. 1 covering 73 acres constructed by T. A. Walker, between 1884 and 1889, gave access on its east side to Dock No. 2 with 34 acres, constructed 1894-1898 by Price and Wills. The Lady Windsor Lock which permitted traffic regardless of the state of the tide was built between 1893 and 1898. The port, linked by the Barry Railway to the coalfield, was in its heyday between 1889 and 1914. Coal exports rose from three millions in 1890 to eleven millions by 1913, the latter being a world record for the export of coal from one port. In the Great War the docks played its part by the shipment of large quantities of coal for the British and Allied Governments and in the loading of large transports with supplies for the armies abroad. The majority of the pictures in this section were taken by Heber Shirvington (1870-1960) who had established his studio at 77 Main Street, Cadoxton, by 1909 and continued to live there for half a century. He had been in partnership with his father, a professional photographer in Bristol, before coming to Barry in 1889 where he initially found work in the graving docks. This and his great love for the sea account for his interesting pictures, many of which have only recently come to light

160   Barry Island looking towards Sully Wood. Work is in progress on constructing the eastern coffer dam in the winter of 1884/5. A small contractors' engine is in the foreground. Vertical steam boiler cranes and 'sheer legs' are at work on the wall. The dam was closed 2 July, 1885

161 The west dam between the Island and mainland was closed in March 1886 after several abortive attempts. T. A. Walker's navvies in the summer of 1886 are digging out the dock with the aid of vertical boiler excavators which put the earth into spoil wagons fitted with dumb buffers

162 Mrs Lewis Davis (dressed in white) preparing to cut the ceremonial silken ribbon of red, white and blue, seconds before the S.S. *Arno* the first ship to enter the dock steamed into the Basin. The placards read 'Welcome to all Nations' 'Success to Barry Docks'

163 This view looking west shows work on the junction cut, a waterway running between Docks Nos. 1 and 2. The line of empty spoil wagons wait to be filled with excavated material by the steam crane before it is hauled away by the *Runcorn*, the contractors' steam locomotive driven by Thomas Sandall

164 Bed of Dock No. 2 from the west. The contractors, Messrs. Price and Wills, began work in 1894 and the dock covering 34 acres was opened on Monday 10 October 1898. Access was through the east side of Dock No. 1. The small contractors' engine and trucks are near the south wall. The ramp is situated where the Geest boats now unload

165 The Lady Windsor Lock constructed between 1893 and 1898 permitted traffic to enter the dock regardless of the state of the tide. This is a facility provided in the Bristol Channel solely by Barry. Dignitaries are standing on the bed at the official opening on 4 January 1898. The masts belong to a sailing ship in Dock No. 1

166 Before the opening in 1898 of the grand General Docks Offices designed in the Neo-Classic style by Arthur E. Bell, the administrative offices of the Barry Railway and Dock Company was this wooden hut. It was erected opposite Ward the Butcher and the *Barry Dock Hotel* (popularly called the 'Chain Locker'), Dock View Road

167 Barry Dock No. 1 in the early 1890s crammed with sailing ships. The port was soon known the world over and the low level coal hoist on the mole (on right) is loading coal into the *Charlie Baker*, Yarmouth New York. The dredger *David Davies* is in the left corner

168 Coal trimmers level coal in the holds of a ship *c*.1905. They were employed by David Davies & Son of Ferndale and are loading coal at No. 17 low level tip on the mole

169 Barry Dock *c*.1905. The stern of a ship is in the front dock of the Barry Graving Dock and Engineering Co. The dock was built as a private contract by T. A. Walker at the same time as Dock No. 1, and opened on the same date in 1889

170 Barry Dock *c*.1905 looking towards the Docks Offices shows a steamship being manoeuvred with the help of tugs in a dock crowded with steam and sailing ships. A Barry Railway class F saddletank engine is shunting on the south side where pit wood is being unloaded

171   The nearest sailing ship is in the Lady Windsor Lock. Ships are visible on the east side of the Basin near the timber sheds belonging to Meggitt & Jones. Three signal boxes controlling trains shunting across the dock are also in view

172   This view is taken looking across Dock No. 1 to Meggitt & Jones' timber sheds on the east side of the Basin. On the right is the Basin entrance to the dock

173 A view taken from a ship in Dock No. 1 looking south to C. H. Bailey's Commercial Dry Docks. In the foreground painted with the letters B.R. is one of the Barry Railway's smaller dock wagons. The twin funnels on the left belong to a Red Funnel steamer in the Basin

174 Ships moored in the tier of Dock No. 1. In the background is the chimney of the hydraulic engine house, Barry Island. The *Tredegar Park*, nearest the camera, has a 'turret-deck' design to reduce toll charges on ships using the Suez Canal where toll was charged on the deck area

175 This picture is taken from the deck of a ship looking along the high level tips of the north side of Dock No. 1 with the Graving Dock and Sully in the distance

176 View from a coal tip on the north side of the mole looking across Dock No. 1 to the high level coal hoists with the town and Docks Offices in the distance. The ship marked with S on the funnel is a 'turret-deck'

177 The *Tuskar* is loading coal on the south side of Dock No. 1 while the *Trident* is waiting her turn. Her Newcastle registration is interesting as it relates to the establishment of the famous 'Ports-to-Ports Express' in which ships' crews were moved by rail between Barry and Newcastle. The service was inaugurated in May 1906

178 View from the west side of Dock No. 1 looking across the mole which is lined with 'Cambrian' and 'Insoles' coal wagons. Coal hoists are on the south side of the Dock. On the left is the giant 50 ton crane and the chimney of the now demolished hydraulic engine house

179 A fixed jib three ton hydraulic crane on the south side of Dock No. 2 unloading meat carcasses from the *Highland Laird*, into the Cold Stores. G.W.R. Mica vans are outside the stores. Rank's mill is in progress of construction in this picture *c.*1904

180 Cranes unloading pit wood on the south side of Dock No. 2 at its western end. Rail enthusiasts will note the flat bottomed rails in the sidings

181 General Docks Offices with statue of David Davies. The roof of Solly Andrews' Coffee Tavern is on the left. To the right is an accumulator used to keep pressure in the hydraulic pipes that worked the coal hoists, cranes and dock gates

182 View from Redbrink Point looking across Bailey's Commercial Dry Dock and the Lady Windsor Lock to the Dock entrance. Two paddle steamers of the Red Funnel fleet, the *Westonia* minus her funnels undergoing repairs, and the *Gwalia*, are inside the Basin

183 Ships loading with coal at high level tips on the north side of Dock No. 1 with ships in foreground waiting their turn to load during the heyday of the docks in the years before the Great War

184 These ships are in the docks of the Barry Graving Dock and Engineering Co., on the east side of Dock No. 1. The 'back' dock (right) was built on the site of the junction cut to the original timber pond which lay to the north of Dock No. 2

185 Ships unloading coal on the north side of Dock No. 2. The Docks Offices are behind the first tip on the right. The coal tips in the distance are in Dock No. 1 and Battery Road which leads from the Docks to the Island is clearly visible on the left

186 This picture from the top of No. 1 tip in Dock No. 1 is looking east across the dockland with the Barry Graving Dock and Engineering Co., in the foreground. The rails on the left have been replaced by a modern road. The distant coal tips are sited on the north side of Dock No. 2

187 Barry Dock No. 1 in 1911 looking east to Rank's Mill in the distance. The dock is crammed with ships two years before the world record tonnage of 11 million tons of coal from one port were exported in 1913

188 Barry Dock in 1911. Ships are closely packed together in the tier of Dock No. 1. Behind their masts are the Docks Offices (left) and Rank's Mill (near centre)

189 These small locomotives with chalked up nicknames *Nancy, Betsy*, etc., are seen under the giant 50 ton hydraulic crane on the south side of Dock No. 1 waiting their turn for shipment to the continent during the 1914-18 war

190 The *War Cowslip* a large camouflaged transport loading in the west end of the south side of Dock No. 2 during the Great War. She has a mounted gun on the stern. On the deck are quick release floats for use in case the ship was sunk

191 The *Oxfordshire*, a hospital ship, is manoeuvring with the aid of tugs in Dock No. 1 during the Great War. The first V.A.D. hospital in Wales was opened at Barry and with a total of 437 beds in the town Barry had a larger number of beds per 100 of the population than any town in Wales

192 The pier branch line of the Barry Railway Company terminated alongside the passenger pontoon. The paddle steamer *Gwalia* of the company's short-lived Red Funnel Line is moored alongside the pontoon and their single funnel paddle steamer *Barry* is approaching

193 The footpath (now closed) from Redbrink Crescent to the Pier Head station was opened in 1908 by the Barry Railway Co., for use of passengers. Campbell's White Funnel Steamer *Waverley* is approaching the pontoon. Brixham trawlers are moored in the dock entrance in this pre-Great War picture

PASSENGER BOATS
BARRY DOCK

194 The paddle steamers of the Red Funnel Fleet are pictured *c*.1908 at their winter moorings in the basin. The *Westonia* is nearest the camera and beyond it are the *Devonia* and *Gwalia*. The single funnel steamer *Barry* is on the right

195 The P.S. *Gwalia* is tied up alongside the Passenger Pontoon with the single funnel *Barry* alongside. The Barry Company's running powers were so curtailed by restrictions the steamers made a financial loss and were all sold by December 1911. The *Gwalia* was sold in May 1910 to the Barrow-in-Furness Railway

BARRY PLEASURE STEAMERS

196 Paddle steamers owned by P. & A. Campbell first called at Barry Pier in July 1899 and resumed calling there after the failure of the Red Funnel Fleet. This picture of the early 1930s shows the P.S. *Cambria* mooring at the Passenger Pontoon. The Barry Island pleasure boat the *Silver Queen* (left) was lost at Dunkirk

197 This picture of the Bristol Channel Pilot Cutters Race in September 1906 was taken from Nell's Point and shows the cutters racing across Whitmore Bay past Friar's Point. The letters CF and NT on the sails signify the Cardiff and Newport cutters respectively

198/199 There was a rare attraction for thousands of Barry holidaymakers on Wednesday morning 25 August 1926 when the Italian steamer *Valsesia* bringing coal to Barry from South America during the General Strike ran aground in dense fog on the head of Friar's Point. As the tide receded the vessel settled down on its jagged bed and broke its back. Hundreds flocked to Barry Island to pilfer coal and a number made court appearances. The cargo was discharged into lighters. After several attempts salvage was completed on Friday evening 22 October when the Cornish Salvage Co. scuttled the broken wreck on Whitmore Bay

200 The German steamer *Walkure* of Hamburg turned turtle on the morning of Thursday 13 August 1908 while loading bunkers under No. 28 tip Dock No. 2. She was on her way from the Baltic with a huge cargo of deals for Natal and as the trucks of coal were being tipped into the hold she suddenly lurched to port. Fortunately as she heeled over her iron masts caught on the side of the steamer *Trevessa*. Providentially not one person drowned or was buried by loose coal and the few injuries sustained were not serious